# ALL ASIAN FOOTBALL MAGAZINE

# FOOTBALL WAR IN THE MIDDLE EAST

It is with great pleasure that we present to our readers the first issue of All Asian Football Magazine, a new project that will focus on different regions of Asia, exploring football, economic and social issues linked to our favorite sport.

In this first release we decided to focus our attention on the Arabian Peninsula, exploring the political diatribe that has been going on since 2017, when Saudi Arabia and the other Gulf monarchies decided to end diplomatic relations with Qatar. Doha has been accused of supporting terrorism, as it is closer, politically speaking, to Shiite Iran, the great enemy of Riyadh.

For over a decade, the Arab states, through the richest sovereign wealth funds, have started investing in football by changing the balance of power on a global level, in a way that Russia and China have not yet managed to accomplish. The Emirs' Manchester City and Qatar's Paris Saint Germain have overturned the European transfer market by raising the bar more and more every year, up to the over 200 million euros that the Parisians spent to snatch Neymar from Barcelona. These aggressive maneuvers have led to a surge in the price of the players transfer prize, but for the two 'Arab clubs' there are consequences to pay: Manchester City was banned by UEFA to partecipate to European Cups for the next two years having violated the Financial Fair Play, and Paris Saint Germain could be the next club to be banned.

The biggest controversy in world football was the assignment of the World Cup in Qatar, an unexpected event that put the small Gulf state at the center of global attention. In recent years, tourism and foreign direct investment in Qatar have increased, but at the same time, the risks of this great media exposure have brought to light many controversies that undermine the image of Qatar: from the accusations of terrorism by the Saudi Arabia, up to the investigations on the corruption for the assignment of the World Cup and the countless deaths on the construction sites of the stadiums.

Saudi Arabia is the last major actor who has decided to invest in the entertainment and sports sector. After years of isolation, Crown Prince Mohammed Bin-Salman's reforms want to bring Riyadh to a new dimension and football is also part of this plan: organization of international sporting events such as the Formula E Grand Prix, or the Super Cups of Italy and Spain, and also the acquisition of Clubs, with the Royal Family Fund close to taking control of a historical team like Newcastle United in England.

The three most important countries of the Gulf area, Saudi Arabia, Qatar and UAE, seek to use football entertainment in general as a vehicle to improve their image in the public eye and take advantage of new economic opportunities, thus becoming key players in the global economy, in order to become independent from oil in the long term, through investments in strategic sectors such as automotive, banks and luxury brands. Football therefore also becomes a battleground between the states of the Arabian Peninsula: in recent times, the Qatari state broadcaster BeIn has asked the Premier League control committee to block the acquisition of Newcastle as Saudi Arabia hacking the signal of BeInSports, illegally transmits the English championship in the Arabian Peninsula.

In this first issue of All Asian Football Magazine, we will explore the economic, political and social issues of football in the Arabian Peninsula and the Middle East in general. In the first section we will analyze the investments in European football, the benefits and risks. The second part 'Football and Society' we dedicated a focus on the women's football movement in the various Arab states, and we also talked about the rebirth of football in Yemen, a country afflicted by a long civil war, whose national team, despite everything, took part in the last Asian Cup. The third part is dedicated to the keyrole people: we will analyze the Saudi entertainment minister Turki Al-Sheikh, owner of Almeria, and Omar Abdulrahman, the 'Maradona of the Desert'. The last part will be dedicated to the best teams of 2019: the Qatar National team winner of the Asian Cup and Al-Hilal, who triumphed in the AFC Champions League.

The Authors of the Magazie (in alphabetical order)

**Accorroni Eduardo** (@ Zaratus34) - Al-Hilal: the Asian club of the century

**Focardi Dario** (@dariofocardi) - Arab investments in European Football

**Gemmi Lugi** (@Luisgemmi) - What are the plans of Turki Al-Sheikh / Atlas of the names of Arab football

**Gineprini Nicholas** (@allafcfootball) - Aspire Generation / Numbers and statistics

**Javadi Saman** (@samanjavadi) - "UAE are better then England" said Amoory

**Ricotta Mattia** (@mattiaricotta) - Yemen's Football reborn

**Servadei Danilo** (@daniloservadei) - Women's football in the Arabian Peninsula

Thanks to **Franco Ficetola** (@ Franco92C14) who designed the cover of All Asian Football Magazine

*SOCIAL MEDIA* 

You can follow All Asian Football on Facebook and Twitter (@allafcfootball), also find us on Mixcloud and Spreaker where we upload our Podcasts

*WEBSITE* 

www.allasianfootball.com

CONTACTS 

allasianfootball@gmail.com

**INDEX**

# An *overview* of *investment* in *Football* by *Arab Investors*

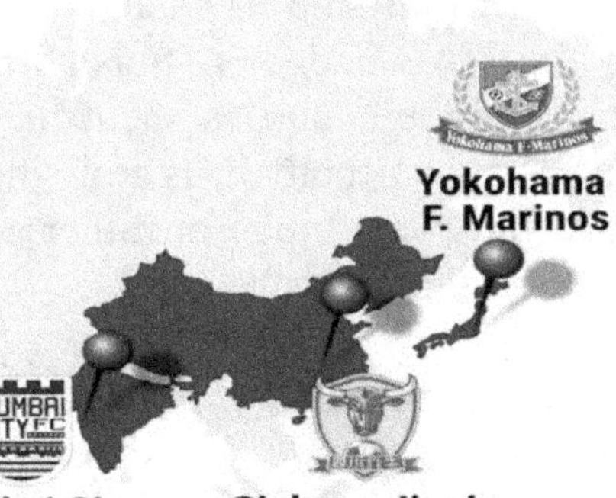

*City Football Group Family - Footballbenchmark.com*

# Arab Investments in European Football

## A direct way to take a place in the heart of Football Entertainment

uk.reuters.co

Take a plane with me, obviously respecting the sanitary conditions that the moment requires, and we will fly to three of the richest countries on the planet. We will first stop in Qatar, continue our travels in the UAE and then finish it in Saudi Arabia. These three countries spent hundreds of millions of euros on football. Is it a sincere love for the sport that we all love or rather a strategic plan that hides other goals?

Football is an extraordinary passion capable of moving billions of people but which carries all the stylistic features of a big business. "It's capitalism, baby," quoting a famous mockumentary by American director Michael Moore. FIFA, the most represented international football body, is one of the most important holding companies on the planet. Its president, the Italian-Swiss Gianni Infantino, admitted that the organization has a treasury of 2.4 billion euros to spend. In 2018 its revenue was 4.2 billion euros, with a profit of around 1.5 billion euros. Much of this economic success is due to the excellent results achieved by the 2018 World Cup which took place in Russia and which went beyond all expectations.

While I am flying over the Mediterranean I open the airline's free magazine and see the logo of the 2022 World Cup and below the Chinese FIFA sponsors, from Dalian Wanda to Hisense. China has been a major investor in world football. A soft power strategy that has brought famous players and coaches to the eastern country, as well as heavy investments for the purchase of European teams. Then, from 2019, the Chinese government has decided to put a stop to this expansion, blocking sporting investments abroad. This has ensured other important investors already present in European football to have free ground after seeing a contest disappears. If we dig deeper and take a closer look at the relationship between the countries of the Arabian Peninsula and the Chinese state, we realize that, as far as investments in the sports sector are concerned, they are closely linked. China has officially stepped back but under track it continues to invest heavily in major international sporting events through important partnerships.

I look out the window. I landed in Doha, the capital of Qatar, the first stop on our tour. The trip you are going to do with me in will be among exotic places, numbers, football, politics and sport washing in the three richest nations of the Arabian Peninsula. Three absolute monarchies, in which social and civil rights are very far from being reality. I still have a final premise to make for you. What do I mean by sport washing? To explain it, I borrow the words of Simon Chadwick, a professor at the University of Nottingham and one of the leading experts on the subject: "It is the use of the sports field, creation or participation in world-class events, by authoritarian regimes with wide-ranging projects that involve host countries and their citizens to clean up their image and distract those same citizens from the continuous violations of rights that take place within their borders ".

## QATAR

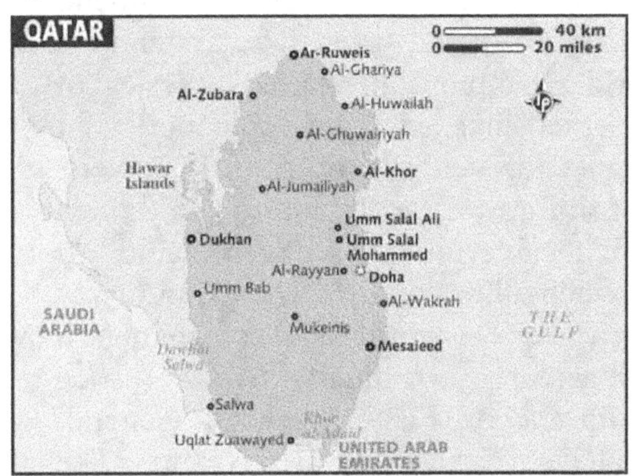


Lonelyplanet.com

Population: 2,350,000 inhabitants
Capital: Doha
Surface: 11,437 sq km
Form of government: Constitutional monarchy
Re: Emir Tamir Bin Hamad Al Thani
Prime Minister: Abdullah Bin Nasser bin Khalifa Al-Thani
Growth rate: 4.93%

We arrive in Doha and it's definitely chilli. Strange, isn't it? Air conditioning is the friend you can rely on to survive these latitudes during the summer heat. Despite these climatic contraindications, the next soccer world cup will be played in Qatar, even if it will be done in December. It is in these conditions that the World Athletics Championships were held last September between empty stadiums, organizational problems and athletes collapsed on the ground during the marathon. The controversial assignment of the football World Cup to the detriment of England and the United States meant that on that day all the fans began to realize the power of a small country in front of the Persian Gulf that until that time didn't have a relevant sports history. Why did Qatar decide to invest with such force in the world of football? Let's try to understand it by dividing the issue into two topics, the sports and the political.

**The ramifications in European Football**

Spain has been under Arab rule for many centuries and their civilization has left indelible artistic marks. This is why the first Qatari intervention in professional football takes place in Spain. We are in 2010 and Sheikh Abdullah bin Nasser bin Abdullah Al Ahmed Al Thani buys Malaga FC, a team that plays in La Liga. The sporting results are immediately interesting, in the 2012/2013 season, the Andalusian team manages to arrive in the Champions League after a brilliant 4th place. But it's a straw fire because since the following year the situation becomes explosive. The Qatari owner makes it very clear that he is there to win the contract for the construction of new infrastructure in nearby Marbella, a 400,000,000 euro deal. But despite this the Ayuntamiento malague does not grant the contract. The sheikh keeps his promise and the team is dismantled, while never completely disengaging.

In the distance, i can see a torch-shaped tower, casting its shadow on the Aspire sports center, the largest indoor academy in the world that gave birth to the National selection that became the Asian champion in 2019 and which will have to perform well at the 2022 World Cup. Qatar has expanded its influence in European football thanks also to the Aspire Foundation, acquiring clubs such as Kas Eupen in Belgium and Cultural Leonesa in Spain as well as forging partnerships with Lask Link and Leeds United in order to loan the main youth talents to complete their training process.

We are at the beginning of the summer of 2011 and while we are relaxing at the sea, Paris St. Germain is purchased by Qatar Sport Investments (QSI), the subsidiary of the Qatar Investement Autority (QIA), the investment fund that directly belongs to Emir Abdulla bin Mohammed bin Saud Al-Thani, distant relative of the president and owner of Malaga. The keyrole person for this operation is the president of QSI, the 47-year-old businessman and former Qatari tennis player, Nasser Al-Kelaifi. The businessman has made a career within the monarchist regime and today takes on many important positions: he is minister without portfolio of the Arab state, President and CEO of the beIN Media Group and President of the Parisian team. Why exactly Paris St. Germain? A medium-cabotage team up to that time, but a city where to build a work base in one of the most important political-economic capitals in Europe and improve its image, create new political and economic relations at a time when Qatar was starting to be listed as one of the financiers of some terrorist groups.

In the meantime, the investments have continued incessantly: the beIN Media Group (formerly known as Al-Jazheera Sport), the media arm of the QSI, has invested 200 million euros to acquire the television rights of Ligue 1, while the football club has started purchases international stars bringing to the Parc des Princes, players of the caliber of Zlatan Ibrahimovic, Edison Cavani, Angel Di Maria, Kirian Mbappe and obviously Neymar. Suddenly all this overexposure has started to arouse the indignation of many international media.

In conjunction with the purchase of the Brazilian player, Saudi Arabia and the other countries of the Arabian Peninsula have broken off relations with the Qatariot emirate because, according to their information, Doha had become the basis for Hamas' terrorist activities. A sort of unexpected short circuit for those who are familiar with the Arab-Islamic world because the organization we are talking about is Palestinian, and cannot be traced back to the Al-Qāʿida network. Why then was Qatar isolated from its Arab neighbours? The political and diplomatic expansion that the small Gulf state managed to achieve in a very short time were succesfull and bothered its most powerful neighbours, Saudi Arabia at the head, because they questioned age-old balances. The second reason concerns how the World Cup was awarded and the nation that came out defeated, the United States, which do not welcome the friendly relations between Iran and Qatar.

**The controversial World Cup**

*Global launch for official Qatar 2022 World Cup emblem -en.as.com*

Qatar enters in the map of football fans on December 2nd 2010. Today we know that that assignment of the world cup was at least controversial and various directors of the FIFA board have been convicted or are investigated for bribery, like the former President. plenipotentiary, Joseph Blatter. The assignment of the world championship started a series of investments that changed the foreign policy of the small state forever. But from great powers, great responsibilities arise. Trying to avoid them through illicit subterfuge is not acceptable. At the time when the covid-19 pandemic was exploding all over the world, Nasser Al Khelaifi was investigated by ordinary Swiss justice together with the ex FIFA Secretary General, Jerome Valcke (barred for 10 years). The accusation is of corruption and incorrect management of the announcement for the concession of the television rights of the next world championship and the subsequent Confederations Cup. Al Khelaifi, through one of his companies bought a house in Costa Smeralda for the FIFA manager. Overall, this game would have saved or earned Valcke, it depends on how you look at it, about 1,800,000 euros.

In June 2019, former UEFA president Michel Platini was placed in pre-trial detention and interrogated following investigations by the European Investigation Consortium. According to the reconstructions of the investigative newspaper Mediapart, on November 2010, the

French presidential palace, the Elysée, hosted a table at which sat Michel Platini, the Crown Prince Al Tani, as well as Claude Gueant, secretary of the Elysée. Exactly nine days before the assignment of the World Cup, the fate of European football was decided: Micheal Platini would have guaranteed his vote to Qatar, and in exchange the QIA would have purchased Paris Saint Germain and invest in the Legardere Group.

As we reach the center of the futuristic Qatari capital, sitting in the back seat of the cool and comfortable taxi, our gaze stops on the sports facilities under construction and we notice the hundreds of migrant workers who struggle under the scorching heat. Safety conditions are an accessory norm reluctantly accepted by large companies. Here we are at off-scale levels. Thousands of Nepalese, Filipinos and Indians move on the scaffolding flooded by the desert sun. We know that they are exploited. It's called Kafala Systemand it is a sort of internship in which the owner of a company acts as a tutor to every single worker he hires. The owner becomes the master and this allows him to seize the passport of the worker who is thus a real prisoner. In 2016, the Qatari government declared that it had abolished this revolting practice but in fact it is still used today by companies that work on construction sites in the world. We are facing a real slavery. A word that many think outdated but which is practiced in many areas of the world, even the most unsuspected as we will see later.

The 2022 Qatar World Cup will go through despite everything, the big sponsors who have decided to put their brand on the most important world sporting event will not allow the road map to be further modified, pandemic permitting. But from external observers we have to ask a question: are we willing to accept that fundamental social achievements for a democratic society are canceled or suspended? It is with this weight in my heart that I go to the airport and continue my journey. If my first stop has put so much strain, what awaits me in the others?

## UAE

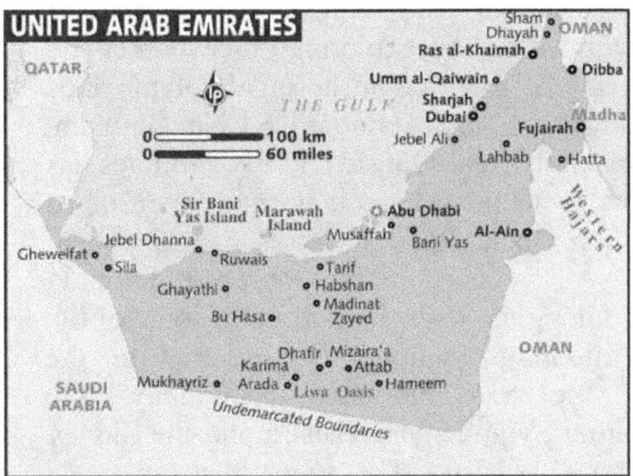



*Lonelyplanet.com*

Population: 9,701,315 inhabitants
Capital: Abu Dhabi
Surface: 83,600 sq km
Form of government: Federal elected absolute monarchy
Re: Khalifa bin Zayed Al Nahayan
Prime Minister: Mohammed bin Rashid Al Maktun
Growth rate: 4.93%

The arrival in Abu Dhabi is less mundane than the previous one. There is a lot of police. They stop me and check my things. They are abrupt but they let me go shortly thereafter. Everything is very controlled. We are talking about one of the most repressive monarchies on the planet. Nothing is left to chance. The UAE is a confederate state. There are seven emirates that make it up: Abu Dhabi, Dubai, Ajman, Fujairah, Ras al-Khaimah, Sharjah and Umm al-Quwain. The emirates of Dubai and Abu Dhabi are the only ones with veto power on legal issues and the two share the management of political power, the monarch is from Abu Dhabi while the prime minister is from Dubai. I am accompanied to see the local attractions as I begin to study how this combination of countries has decided to put football among their desires.

### From Fly Emirates to City Football Group

Apparently the Emirati intervention in sport was not born as a national strategic political choice. The first protagonist is the only Emirate of Dubai and has as its ram head the airline of the emirate's flag, Fly Emirates, which over the years has made lasting partnerships with the main European clubs. Starting from 2004 with

Arsenal (until acquiring the naming rights of the gunners' stadium) and then branching out into Italy with Milan and exploring other markets by sponsoring SL Benfica, in Portugal, Olympiakos FC, in Greece, and Hamburg SV in Germany and especially Real Madrid CF. Fly Emirates has interests in tennis where it is main sponsor of Australian Open, Roland Garros and US Open and 60 ATP events, main sponsor of Formula 1, and among the main supporters of some of the most important symphony orchestras in the world, the San Francisco Symphony, the Melbourne Symphony Orchestra and the Sidney Symphony Orchestra. The project that foresees a repainted facade of the emirates with a vision of a broad perspective that links sport and culture. Yet partnerships alone could not have been sufficient for the political ambitions of the leaders of the Arab country, so we moved on to what we can call a more aggressive phase 2, direct acquisition.

*Twitter.com – @citychief*

On September 1, 2008, Abu Dhabi United Group (ADUG) of Emirate Prince Mansur bin Zayd Al Nahyan bought Manchester City FC from Thai tycoon Thaksin Shinawatra. The prince assumes the position of honorary president while the most operational position ends up on the shoulders of his collaborator Khaldoon al Mubarak. Investments in what is then the other Manchester team are huge right from the start. The goal was to bring Citizens in the elite of British football first and European then in the shortest time possible. The sporting and economic impact of the Emirates' entry into British football has been very strong. On the field they purchased great players like Tevez, Aguero, De Bruyne, Kompany and coaches like Mancini and Guardiola. The numbers spent forced everyone else to raise the bar. An example? The sponsorship agreement that Etihad Airlines has signed with the team to put its name on the stadium and which also includes a substantial sponsorship agreement for the club. The ten-year deal, which started in the 2011/12 season and will end with the 2020/2021 season, has brought about £ 600 million into the company's coffers. Many European clubs primarily the British ones, have always looked suspiciously at this sponsorship that seemed to violate the rules of Financial Fair Play wanted by the then UEFA President, Michel Platini.

In 2014 ADUG founded a holding company, the City Football Group (CFG). Taking Manchester City as the point of the sports pyramid, the new holding has the task of managing the entire network of clubs and the other sports projects that make up the rest of the pyramid. A decidedly more ambitious idea than that implemented by the Qatari neighbours. The Emirates have understood how important it is to have a center that controls the periphery, because important numbers in terms of quality and skills of the people involved can flow from the periphery. Thus under the auspices of the CFG various teams end, some totally controlled like Melbourne City FC, which plays in the Australian A-League, the Montevideo City Torque, which plays in the Primera Division Profesional in Uruguay, the Lommel SK, in the Belgian Second Division, while in Asia also minority shares on Yokohama F. Marinos (Japanese first division), Mumbai City (Indian Super League) and Sichuan Jiuniu (Chinese Third division). The direct or indirect management of all these companies makes it possible to move the players from one to the other without having the problem of normal trading. It is a real multinational company that has little to do with the romantic idea of football that many have in mind. There is one last curiosity , the CFG is not completely in the hands of ADUB, which holds 78% of the shares. Minority shareholders include Silver Lake Partners, a US private equity firm , Citic Capital and China Media Capital, two Chinese national companies.

## The FFP and UEFA's intervention

As in all the stories of this trip, if we turn the corner to shelter from the sun we go into a deep darkness, so it also happens for this stage in the

UAE. The darkness is FFP, a threat that many clubs had tried to launch against the CFG but that had never found an answer in the top of European football. Then something changed. On February 14, 2020, the Club Financial Control Body (CFCB) banned Manchester City from any European competition for 2 years for violating the parameters of the FFP. The charge is that of illegally inflating the revenue from sponsorships. The Citizens will be forced to pay 30,000,000 euro fine.

It would have been difficult to do otherwise after Der Spiegel reported many documents on the matter, starting from emails and confidential documents. The City board immediately appealed to the Sports Arbitration Court (CAS). A move that has substantially frozen the ban decision and which, absurdly, could allow the team to participate in the next 2020/2021 Champions League in the event that the Court's ruling times are prolonged. According to documents published by the German newspaper, Sheikh Mansour, in 2012 and 2016, would have financed almost all of the 70,000,000 euros per year of the team's sponsorship through his company, Abu Dhabi United, and not through Etihad. A procedure deemed illegal by the rules governing the FFP. The CFG has stated that it will continue to manage the City and the whole group connected to it. But what if players and technicians decide to abandon the boat that is staying in the port?

## SAUDI ARABIA

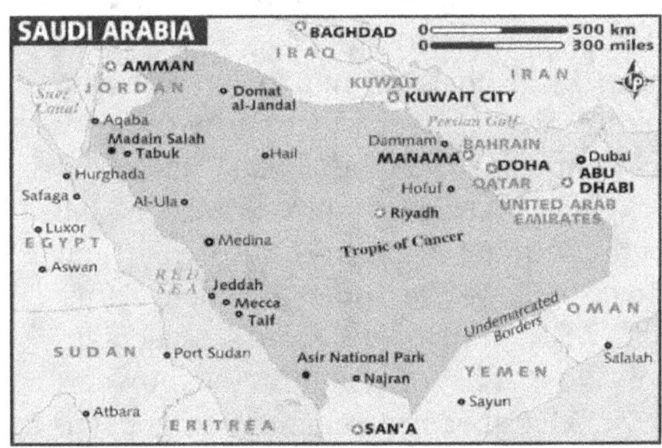


lonelyplanet.com

Population: 31.521.418 inhabitants
Capital: Riad
Surface: 2,149,690 sq km
Form of government: Islamic absolute monarchy
Re: Salman
Prime Minister: -
Growth rate: 1.523%

We have reached the last stage of our virtual journey. This time we stop in Riyadh, the capital of Saudi Arabia, the largest state of the Arabian peninsula. Saudi Arabia is one of the most closed and conservative absolute monarchies on the planet where the Laws of the Guardians are followed, a code of conduct that strictly follows certain dictates of the Koran and which imposes the decisions of older male family members, the "guardians" , to other family members.

It must be said that some timid openness has been seen for some years. In 2017, the Saudi government reopened the cinemas and allowed the two sexes to stay close in public spaces, even if they must belong to the same family. In 2018, after decades in which women were subjected to continuous impediments to gain their own autonomy and independence from family and marriage, thanks to the birth of the Women to drive Movement, the Saudi central government had to give women the opportunity to drive without the presence of men. In the same year, during the Italian Super Cup between Juventus FC and AC Milan, women were admitted to the stadiums although they were unable to mix with men. In 2019, the possibility of travelling abroad was guaranteed without the consent of the guardian of the family for women over 21 years of age. These reforms stem from a precise political vision, the Saudi Vision 2030, which has its maximum expression in the figure of the crown prince Mohammed bin Salman.

### Saudi Vision 2030

The dossier is conspicuous and explains in depth what are the assets in which Saudi Arabia will invest in the coming years to diversify its economy, until now based almost entirely on the revenues from oil processing. The main reason for this change of course lies in the contraction in the price that crude oil suffered after the economic crisis of 2011. In the vision of the Saudi establishment the next pillars on which the development of the nation should be based should be the promotion of a different image of the kingdom outside to be implemented through the development of the education system, the improvement of infrastructure, the modernization of the army, incentives for the use of renewable energies, the creation of new sustainable mobility, the privatization of the electricity, water, hospital, airport sector, the launch of an entertainement sector and tourism and the birth of an international sports policy. In the midst of the dozens of data and graphics in the dossier, which masterfully illustrate the dozens of investments and ideas that are in the 92 pages of the pdf, there is a Pharaonic project, the construction of the perfect city of NEOM, a real megacity conceived as a free zone.

*Richest football club owners - tribuna.com*

One of the most interesting parts of Saudi Vision 2030 is the attempt by the Wahabi monarchy to renegotiate with the religious class some of the prerogatives that it continues to take on, such as school education. This will be one of the crucial issues that Crown Prince Mohammed bin Salman will have to solve. It will not be easy. The connections between temporal and religious power in Saudi Arabia seem similar to those found in medieval Europe. To this are added dark events such as the death of Jamal Ahmad Kashoggi, editor of the Saudi progressive newspaper Al-Watan. The journalist, who was in voluntary exile in Turkey, one morning shows up at the consulate of his country in Istanbul and does not come out alive. Under the pressure from the international community, the Saudi government was forced to admit that Kashoggi had been killed. And also, how can we forget the intervention of the Wahabi army in the civil war in Yemen, a state located in the extreme southwest of the Arabian Peninsula, which has killed thousands of civilians? Once

again, as for Qatar and the UAE, football seems to be the Trojan horse to win the trust of the media and western citizens.

**The International expansion**

To support the change of pace in the domestic sports economy, the Saudi government has broadened its horizons by deciding to invest also internationally. Here comes the second name to keep in mind when one tries to understand what is moving in Saudi Arabia in football, that of Turki Al Sheikh, Ministry of the Entertainment and maximum government manager for sport and association of Prince Mohammed bin Salman. Al Sheikh is a man who has built up a network of very strong international ties. In particular, he has a direct relationship with the current FIFA President, Gianni Infantino, whom he supported during his last election. It is thanks to this special bond that Saudi Arabia decided to invest heavily in the first FIFA Club World Cup which was due to take place in China next summer but which was moved to an indefinite date between 2021 and 2023, for obvious health reasons. Turki Al Sheikh, current entertainment minister, was the owner of Pyramids FC in Egypt and then, after a somewhat turbulent experience, gave up his investment and migrated to Spain, where he took control of Almeria.

The last step that was missing for the Saudi government to show itself even more decisively to the world was the entry into the coolest football league of the current football scene, the English Premier League. As already evident from previous sports investments, even these operations in England seem not to be part of a well-defined project, such as that carried out by neighbours from Qatar and the UAE. Prince Abd Allah bin Musa'id Al Sa'ud, current head of the Saudi Youth Welfare Authority, buys Sheffield United. In 2013 he became president after buying 50% of it. Half of the team's ownership remains in the hands of the previous owner, tycoon Kevin McCabe. The cohabitation goes on between ups and downs for a few years then literally explodes when the English partner brings the Saudi prince to court. The accusation is that he received pressure to obtain a discount on the acquisition of the remaining 50% of the shares. The High Court of Sheffield gave reason to the Saudi prince that he found himself the sole owner of the red and white team by paying the remaining half only $ 6,000,000, instead of the $ 75,000,000 requested by McCabe and his family. In addition, the court denied the possibility of appeal.

The other major investment in the Premier League that has been reported in recent weeks concerns the purchase of the entire Newcastle United equity package. In this case, the PIF, the private fund of the Saudi ruling house, took the field. We are talking about a family that has an estimated private equity of 260 billion euros. An amount that was never seen before in football. Behind this operation is the hand of Crown Prince Mohammed bin Salman. We are facing with an event that if it occurs could really change the world football scene. But there are many doubts that this operation will go through. On the one hand there are the right interventions of the humanitarian associations, primarily Amnesty UK which reports that the leaders of the Football Association (FA) are too soft in their selection criteria, on the other there are more strictly geo-political reasons deriving from the diplomatic conflict with Qatar.

The BeIN communication group reported that its broadcast signal on the Arabian Peninsula and North Africa has been pirated and relaunched by the BeoutQ streaming platform and that this would be directly connected to the Saudi government. Mohammed bin Salman rejected these accusations to the sender, declaring that BeoutQ was born between Cuba and Colombia but in November the Arab state was summoned by the European Commission because it has not yet been able to close the offending platform that it transmits from its territory.

Towards Qatar and the UAE, which as for Saudi Arabia certainly do not shine out of respect for civil rights and opposition voices, they have not undergone the same treatment and have entered European football without worries. Perhaps Saudi Arabia represents a decidedly more important danger than its two small neighbours for the entrepreneurial balance of European or world football?

## Conclusions

Maintaining the secularity of the gaze should be the way we deal with the analysis of countries far from our western patterns. We ourselves have often been the protagonists of the limitation of the rights of other peoples. A role that we continue to maintain even in the present, almost with pride. Take the case of Britain itself. In the territory of Her Majesty Queen Elizabeth II there are 136,000 enslaved people, of whom 41% would be children, as shown by a study released by the Walk Free Foundation. Looking deeply at who we are can allow us to better understand who we are facing. Are we so better and different from them?

These three countries, to varying degrees and ways, are influencing our approach to the sporting event. We are faced with a paradigm shift, it is impossible to deny it. If the Americans, with marketing, the heavy entrance of cable TV, the dizzying increase in wages, the branding of every detail have changed our way of living and reading sports at the end of the millennium, this will also happen with what the Arab countries are doing. The creation of hubs where young players can grow on every continent, the acquisition of second-tier teams to be used as an incubator for these young players, the total assimilation between teams and reference media are some of the things we will have to learn to appreciate. If the future is like this, old Europe will have to be ready.
I write these last sentences while I look outside our hotel. The square is teeming with people. Traditionally dressed women, at a safe distance from men, observe children playing. While I am at check-in I greet the Arabian Peninsula for this last time. It is a goodbye, because this land will still have much to tell us. I sit on the plane and open the on-board magazine and read a sentence that strikes me: "Only the future that is still to be written can tell us what awaits us". Flight home. Salah Maleikum Arabia.

*Focardi Dario*

*Saudi Women Get to Be Fans on the Stands With New Soccer Stadium - mideastspots.com*

*Iran football fans support Yemen - baaz.com*

# Female Football in the Arab Peninsula

**How the countries in the area are developing the women's football movement, from Saudi Arabia to Jordan.**

*Saudi Arabia Female Football Team - Coliseum.online*

Both in Europe and in much of the world, women's football has made great strides in recent years. The World Cup played in France last year (won by the USA ed.) was the most striking example, with the maximum competition for women's national teams that had so much follow-up, obtaining a well-deserved success. To date, there are really many countries that boast a women's national football team and this has only increased the interest in competitions that previously were unjustly very marginalized.

Even Asia in this sense is no exception and the strongest women's national team is Japan, with the Nadeshiko capable of climbing to the top of the world in 2011 by beating the USA on penalties. In addition to the Japanese one, the last world championship was also attended by the Chinese selection, the Australian selection, the Thai selection and the South Korean selection and with the exception of the latter, all of them entered the final phase of the competition. As we can see, the countries belonging to East Asia have always stood out. This is because in Western Asia, women's football has always been held back by social and political issues, but something is also changing there. As the title suggests, we will now analyze how women are finally carving out their space in the world of football in the countries of the Arabian Peninsula.

### Female Football in Saudi Arabia

In the past two years, the Italian Super Cup has taken place in Saudi Arabia and the controversies have certainly not been lacking. Both fans, but also professionals, protested against the League's choice to play the Super Cup in the Arab country precisely because of the way the woman is treated in Saudi society. In the 2018 edition, the trophy was contested by Juventus and Milan in Jeddah and in the stadium women had access only to sectors a dedicated to them.

*Aliaseda.com*

Everything has changed in the 2019 edition of the Super Cup, played in Riyadh and won by Lazio, who was right behind Juventus. The Italian League mediated with the Saudi government and managed to get the female audience to have access to all areas of the stadium. A choice that was considered truly historic for Saudi Arabia which began to show signs of openness towards the female world in a purely patriarchal society. Thus we arrive in February 2020, with the Saudi country announcing the birth of the first women's football championship.

A real achievement for Saudi women who were not even allowed to play sports in public. A choice made by Saudi officials that certainly benefits the international image of the country, which has always been seen as ultra-conservative. The news has been received positively by public opinion, although this is only a small step as regards the role of women in Saudi society.
It is well known, in fact, how both socially and politically, women have less weight than men in Saudi Arabia and it will be necessary to continue to struggle to recognize the same rights (some women also ended up in prison for this ed. ). Returning to the world of football, Saudi Arabia has totally convinced itself in opening all the other sectors of the stadium to women and also

in the Saudi Professional League now they can sit anywhere, without any limitations or sectors dedicated to them

As for the women's championship, it should have started in March, but the Coronavirus emergency has effectively blocked everything. The matches will be played in Riyadh, Jeddah and Damman.

**Female Football in Jordan**

Progress has also been made in an important way in Jordan. Compared to Saudi Arabia, the JFA (Jordan Football Association) already has its own women's national team born in 2005 and was supported by Prince Ali Bin Al-Husayn in person who does not miss a team game. And it was thanks to the mediation of the Prince that the national team was later recognized by FIFA a few years later. Since then, the Jordanian women's national team has grown a lot and has also taken part in the qualifications for the Women's World Cup since 2011, although it never qualified for the final phase.

*Fifa.com*

The level of involvement of women in Jordanian football has increased exponentially, now Jordan also has an under-17 and an under-15 women's national team. All thanks also to the passion for the football world of Jordanian women, increasingly attracted to this sport. It was last year that Jordan made a good leap forward from the point of view of women's football. In 2019, in fact, the first women's championship was created in which 7 teams took part (14 teams took part in the first Jordanian Cup) and where a total of 89 games between the league and the cup were played. A real dream come true for Stephanie Al Naber, icon of Jordanian women's football, which had always wanted since 2005 a real football season in her country.

The Jordan Women's Pro-League was a real success and ended with the victory of the Shabab Al Ordon in the play-off against Amman SC 1-0 after the two teams had closed the season on equal points. Match that was repeated also in the cup final and the result was identical, with Shabab Al Ordon who gave himself the first, historic double in the world of Jordanian women's football.

The Jordanian movement is clearly the most advanced, in 2018 it organized the first Women's Asian Cup held in the West of the continent, then won by Japan. On that occasion the Jordanian national team lost all three games in the group against China, the Philippines and Thailand.

**Female Football in UAE**

*The national.ae*

Unlike Jordan, the United Arab Emirates (UAE) do not yet have a women's championship, but since 2010 they have their own national team capable of being immediately victorious. In that year, in fact, the national team won the West Asian Football Federation Women's Championship beating Jordan 1-0 in the final. Success repeated then the following year by defeating Iran on penalties (2-2 after extra time). In addition, to improve their standards, the UAE involved many of their players in cultural exchanges with the United States, but despite everything they failed to qualify for the French World Cup.

As for the championship, as mentioned, there is not one, also because despite the popularity of Emirati women's football, it is played only in the richest areas of the country. The economic condition is not the same for everyone and this currently makes it impossible to create a championship. So where do the women belonging to the Emirate national team come from?

Most of the players are from Abu Dhabi Country Club, one of the most famous sports academies in the country. At the moment, Emirati women's football at club level exists only at school level and it is thanks to the Abu Dhabi Sports Council that progress has been made at national level. In all the UAE 22 sports centers have been opened under the watchful eye of the Abu Dhabi Sports Council which attracted many Emirati girls.

The hope is that in the future the United Arab Emirates may also have their own championship. Meanwhile, Emirati girls can play football thanks to school tournaments and, thanks to the Abu Dhabi Sports Council, they can dream of playing for their national team.

**Female Football in Qatar**

*fifa.com*

For about 8 years, the Qatar worked hard on the female club level. In 2012 the first women's championship was created which in 2014 reached seven teams. Public opinion has always defined the choice to open football to women and young girls as "unusual", Qatar and its football federation have never given up, with the intention of giving a more progressive image of the country regarding binomial women-sport compared to other Arab countries.

Qatar's goal is to bring men's and women's football to the same level and, although there is still much to be done, encouraging signs have arrived. The standard bearer of Qatari women's football is the goalkeeper of the national team Shaima Abdullah who is also a member of the Generation Amazing, a social development program that helps young people to get closer to the world of football. In view of the 2022 World Cup, Qatar is doing everything to show itself a different country than the other states of the Arabian Peninsula, standing almost as a champion of women's rights not only in terms of sport, but also at a social and political level. They return to speaking in purely football terms for the World Cup Qatar is thinking of involving women too, despite the opposition of the most conservative forces in the country who have said they are ready to prevent this.

Speaking of World Cups, a special mention deserves the Qatari women's national team which was founded in 2010 and has never taken part in the maximum competition for women's national teams, nor in the women's Asian Cup. The only participation in a tournament is that of 2014 in the West Asian Football Federation Women's Championship which was played in Jordan, where the Qatari national team came in fourth place.

**Female Soccer in the rest of Arab Peninsula**

*Nazionale femminile del Bahrain - challengesoccer.com*

The other states of the Arabian Peninsula in recent years have also made progress from the point of view of women's football. In Bahrain, the women's national team was founded in 2003 and in 2014 wrote a historical page for the Arab women's movement, becoming the first national team to challenge a European women's national team, facing Italy in Florence on May 17th.

In Yemen women's football started in 2005 when, with the help of FIFA, women were able to get closer to the world of football. The merit was of the FIFA's Financial Assistance Program (FAP), launched in 1998 by the highest international football body, which obliged all the federations to invest 4% of their FAP in women's football. 160 women were registered in the football program launched by Yemen, including 110 adult players and 50 junior players. In 2009, Yemen came to count 9 women's club teams, including 6 seniors and 3 juniors. The national team, however, was recognized by FIFA in 2006, but did not play any game.

In Kuwait, instead, there are seven women's club teams and in 2017 the Kuwait Women's Football League, the first Kuwaiti women's championship. At the level of National, that of Kuwait has never taken part neither in the qualifications for a World Cup, nor in those for the Asian Cup.

Important progress has also been made in Oman where the women's championship has been played regularly since 2016, in which initially eight teams took part. From the next edition, however, the tournament should be extended to all the governorates of the Sultanate. And it will be thanks to the championship that we will also try to shape the national team female, choosing the best players in the country. To date, in fact, there has never been a real Omani women's national team.

*Servadei Danilo*

# Yemen's Football Reborn

***When sport becomes a necessity: today's football situation in Yemen, a country devastated by the civil war***

*Full stands at the final of the national tournament played last January. Source: yemsport.com (Al-Hindi & Ayman Al-Qadi)*

Last March 25th was the fifth anniversary of the outbreak of the Yemen civil war. A conflict in which the parties involved are finally conceiving the word *negotiation* after more than 200 thousand deaths and more than 3 million displaced people. The population is exhausted, so much so that according to a recent report by the United Nations Development Programme (UNDP), continuity of the conflict between now and 2022 would lead Yemen to become the poorest country in the world. The perception that things are starting to change comes not only from the declarations and the deeds of the puppeteers of the massacre, but also from the resumption of some activities almost abandoned for years: this is the case of sport, and particularly football. The most popular competitive activity of the state has been taking place regularly since the end of 2019, which at the beginning of the year saw the return of the local Premier League, after five years.

With the worsening conditions of extreme difficulty that the nation is facing, as evidenced by the UNDP figure which today classifies 65% of Yemenis as extremely poor, and a future that looks equally problematic, sport is now considered not more as a leisure but as a necessity. An instrument of distraction especially for the new generations, whose future is already compromised.

**The context**

Since unification in 1990, Yemen has experienced only a few years of peace, between internal instability and terrorist insurrections. The turning point came in January 2011 when government protests, generated by strong popular discontent over the spread of unemployment and poverty, and attributable to the *Arab Spring* (the series of protests that characterized the Arab world between 2010 and 2012), resulted in a revolution that forced the head of state Ali Abdullah Saleh to resign, after 20 years as president. The political and governmental instability created led the Shiite armed group of the Houthi, in strong opposition to the state for several years, to take advantage of the moment to try to take control of the country, mostly Sunni.

After conquering the northern part of the nation, including the capital Sana'a, the self-described *Supporters of God* arrived in March 2015 at the gates of Aden, the main southern city and temporary new capital, where the official Yemeni government and the new president Abd Rabbuh Mansu Hadi had taken refuge. At this point the civil war began. On the one hand we find the Houthi, who master almost all of northern Yemen, including the capital, with the support of the largest Shiite country, Iran. On the other side there is the official government which still controls the southern and eastern part of the country, and which benefits the strong support of a coalition led by Saudi Arabia, which includes the United States, France and Egypt, between the others.

Furthermore, terrorist groups affiliated to Al-Qaeda and the Islamic State are taking advantage from the situation, controlling vast territories of central Yemen and some coastal cities. But that's not enough. After a series of arguments, in 2017 the former governor of Aden, Aidarus al-Zoubaidi, ousted by the head of state who had taken refuge in the port city two years earlier, decided to separate from the central government and to proclaim the Southern Transitional Council, with the aim of re-establishing the state of South Yemen. To date, the Council, aided by the United Arab Emirates, controls part of the southern areas, including Aden.

So, the complicated civil conflict is currently being fought between four factions. It is easy to understand how the interest in this land goes far beyond the contrasts between the north and south of the country, and between Sunnis and Shiites. Indeed, Yemen's position is highly strategic. Being in the far south of the Arabian Peninsula means seeing millions of tons of goods, especially oil, pass a few kilometres every day. And for regional economic giants (such as Saudi Arabia and Israel) having an allied country in that position means a lot.

In recent months the spread of poverty, the constant pressure of the UN, the huge military and economic effort required and, lastly, the spread of Covid-19, are converging sides towards a first phase of negotiations, which will certainly be long and complicated. And in this situation of strong uncertainty, the reopening of sports facilities, at least those that have not been destroyed or not reused for other tasks (such as serving as military camp), becomes for many Yemenis one of few elements on which to cling to have the strength to keep going.

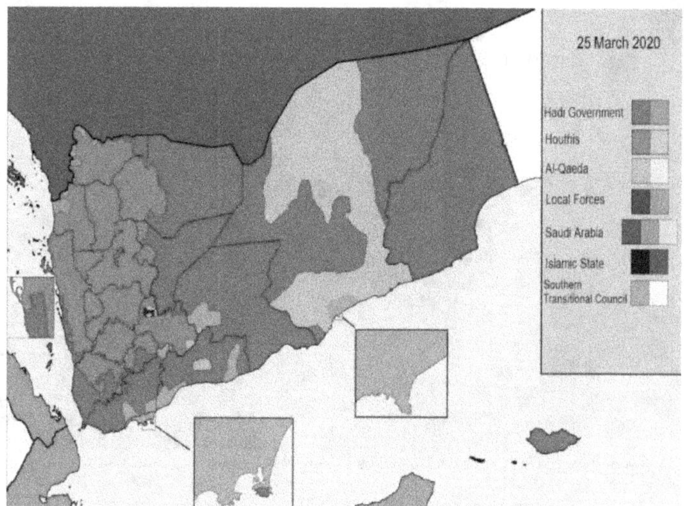


*The Yemeni situation on March 25th, 2020. Source: YouTube/Koopinator*

**The football situation**

With the intensification of the internal crisis, in January 2015 the Yemen League (the first football division) was suspended and then definitively cancelled without the assignment of the title. A few days later a terrifying civil war would begin, which would upset the lives of all Yemenis, including athletes. With the resumption of the championship to date, the life of the players was at a crossroads. Many decided to leave the country to knock on foreign league doors (in particular Qatar, United Arab Emirates, Oman and Malaysia); others managed to continue playing, reconciling participation in local tournaments with a second job; still others were forced to quit, while some decided to enlist. Like the young promise Abdullah Aref, goalkeeper of the Shoala Club, who was killed in a gunfight with the rebels in 2015.

The situation has become almost unsustainable even for the clubs themselves. Three first division teams were literally destroyed: bombed or seized stadiums, looted equipment and damaged facilities. This is what happened to Al-Tilal SC, Al Saqr SC and Al-Yarmuk Al-Rawda, three of the most successful clubs with the best infrastructure in the country. Unfortunately, this fate has also fallen to many minor league companies. Other clubs, on the other hand, were fortunate to be able to continue to keep their facilities open, especially in the central part of the country, the least affected by the conflict. In these areas, the joint effort of the regional detachments of the Yemen Football Association, local governments and wealthy personalities made it possible to organize short but constant competitions, which allowed the Yemeni football movement not to disappear.

**The national team**

Despite the incessant conflict, the national representatives (both the major and the youths) have succeeded, albeit with difficulty, to continue their activities under the same flag with results that are unbelievable. In 2018 the *Red Devils* of Arabia miraculously reached the group stage of the 2019 Asian Cup for the first time in their history. The qualifying campaign was by no means easy. The home games were played at the Qatar SC Stadium in Doha, and for safety reasons the players had to reach the small peninsula by sea, via a two-day journey. The transfers were no different, with the shorter journeys (to Jordan and Saudi Arabia) which lasted at least 48 hours.

On March 27th, 2018 the efforts paid off, and the two goals scored by the young Abdulwasea Al-Matari against Nepal allowed the red devils to get the pass for the Asian Cup. The national team will then finish the competition with zero points, after having played only three friendly preparations throughout 2018 and a handful of training sessions. The most relevant aspect, however, was that in January 2019 the whole nation, from north to south (including military on the front), followed its heroes in the United Arab Emirates, often with makeshift means.

Demonstration of how the national team managed to succeed where the war is miserably failing.

Another important result was achieved by the U-19 football team, which qualified for the next U-19 Asian Cup last November. Returning to Yemen, the boys marched across the country, passing through the capital Sanaa, in the disputed city of Marib and in Aden.

*The Yemeni players celebrate Ethiopian coach Abrham Mebratu at the end of the match against Nepal. Source: news.cn*

**The return of the first division**

Much of the credit for football's survival in these very difficult years goes to the Yemen Football Association. The federation managed to continue operating both in the territories remained under the control of the official Yemeni state and in the northern areas occupied by the Houthi. Thanks to the cooperation with both fronts, the various territorial detachments of the YFA have organized numerous regional tournaments, often in synergy with the local governorates. At the moment almost every region has its own league: ranging from the Winter Forum in Sanaa, to the Bilquis Queen League of Taiz (a city still highly unstable), to the Aden championship, and to the numerous leagues formed in the vast central region of Hadhramaut (whose winners even compete for a super cup).

The great enthusiasm that the major national team and the representative U-19 aroused in 2019, together with the decrease in the intensity of the conflicts, convinced YFA and the Ministry of sport and youth to bring the first division back to life. Between 12 and 24 January 2020, a national tournament comprising eight teams from all over Yemen was held in Seiyun, in

Hadhramaut (one of the most stable regions). The championship was preceded by a territorial qualifying phase in which 34 clubs took part. The finalists were divided into two groups of four teams, followed by the semi-finals and the final. The trophy was won by Al-Shaab Hadhramaut, in their first national title, getting the better of Al-Wahda SC, historical southern club, after the penalty shootout lottery. The Activation League (the official name given to the competition) was a success, above all for the public, with the last match that saw the circular stands of the Olympic Stadium in Seiyun welcoming 30 thousand spectators.

*The award ceremony at the end of the Activation League final. Source: yemsport.com (Al-Hindi & Ayman Al-Qadi)*

As soon as the Activation League ended, the YFA announced its intention to re-establish the normal course of the first two national divisions. The initiative has aroused mixed reactions, above all for the risks that the same teams should face, given that the leagues would be played over the whole country, divided into four. But to date, the project appears blocked. In fact, in the federation's intentions the championships should have started in April, but there is no news on the matter. Probably the strong doubts and the subsequent health emergency linked to covid-19 led to the suspension of the project, at least for the moment. The Yemenis are thus forced to postpone the Yemen League further, but the reborn of football has never been so close.

**Ricotta Mattia**

## The Saudi Ministry of Entertainment and the Maradona of the Desert

*Turki Al Sheikh - english.mubasher.info*

*Omar Abdulrahman a major doubt for UAE's crucial World Cup double-header - thenational.ae*

# What are Turki Al-Sheikh's plans

## The rise in international football of the Saudi Arabia's Ministry of Entertainment

*Turki Al Sheikh, the Saudi's Minitry of Entertainment, owner of Almeria - societytimes.com*

Saudi Arabia is trying to ascend as a football power, and in recent times has achieved commendable results (U19 Asian Champion, U23 Finalist and Al-Hilal winner in the last Champions League), financed in optimal way but completed thanks to a management so far performed in an excellent way.

From the end of the 90s until a few years ago, the country belonging to the Cradle of Humanity, suffered a sort of media diaspora, based mainly on the good of the State, even limiting visits from outside if not for work or pilgrimage (with this last "ban" ended about a year ago), and this is the main cause that for a very long period of time, according to the criteria of the world of football, has made the Saudi macrocosm vanish. Taking the situation in hand and getting back into play after a period of twenty years of absence is never easy, but thanks to the work of the experts, a real football evolution has come.

**The man behind the rise of Saudi sport**

Turki bin Abdulmohsen bin Abdul Latif Al-Sheikh is known primarily as an adviser at the Royal Court of Saudi Arabia and he's currently the highest ministerial authority regarding the whole world of entertainment in the Gulf Monarchy. The young Turki Al-Sheikh finished his studies in 2001 at King Fahd Security College, a prestigious institute located in the east of Riyadh, which makes science and military training its specialty in education . Subsequently, thanks to the weight of the college he attended, fueled by his oratory and organizational skills, he worked in various government sectors including the Ministry of the Interior and the Emirate of Riyadh.

Thus, in 2015 he entered in the organizational structure of the Crown as a councilor, earning the title of Minister of the General Sports Authority in just 2 years, organizing events with a excellent numbers between live viewers and television share, including the Italian Super Cup , the luxury friendly match between Brazil-Argentina, the various WWE stages and Formula-E, where female participation was also allowed. Al-Sheikh's great ability to fit perfectly into the plan of the young Crown Prince Mohammed Bin Salman to revive the international Saudi image, and the various awards received as the most influential personality for the sport in the 2017 and 2018 at the Dubai Conference, took him only one year later to get the keys to Saudi entertainment.

Parallel to the important political position he held, the Minister of Entertainment has decided to start a real entrepreneurial career in the football world. After serving as honorary president of Al-Taawoun in Saudi Pro League and Al-Alhy in Cairo, both of which ended (and started) disastrously, Turki Al-Sheikh arrived in June 2018 as the new owner of the Egyptian club. Al-Assyouti. This parenthesis of the short (for now) career as a corporate chairman of Al-Sheikh is the most curious and intriguing given the modus operandi applied for the very first time in African territories.

**The Pyramids FC experiment in Egypt**

It all started when businessman Mahmoud El-Assyouti decided to sell his club to the Saudi minister. The amount of "only" 5 million dollars, has much deeper roots, as the price included the immediate consolidation of the balance sheet with the consequent debts amounted over the years, due to the disappointing results. As revealed in an interview that El-Assyouti was unable to feel satisfied with the Egyptian system where there were only two sources of revenue: selling players, which allowed the club to be successful, and sponsorship rights, however, only in the First Division. In addition, the main reason that pushed the former chairman to definitively conclude the experience, were the vague statutes and laws that prevent long-term investment plans,

The era of Al-Sheikh as head of Assyouti opened, with general skepticism, given the previous

Egyptian experience at Al-Ahly; in spite of this, the new president decided to dare and implement a total rebranding at his new club. The name, which passed from the obsolete Assyouti Club to the most prestigious Pyramids FC, also implicitly moved the city to which it belonged, migrating from Assiut to the capital of Cairo, with the home games held inside the Stadium named June 30th. Furthermore, a total staff revolution was carried out by changing all sectors, and also the legendary Ricardo la Volpe was hired as the sports director.

*Pyramids FC - director11.com*

The modus operandi could be defined as postmodern, and follows the model of Red Bull, which goes to dismantle the history and the attachment to the club by the fans, killing its roots but investing the capital to obtain results, making the investment valid (albeit selfish), in the shortest possible time. A striking example is Leipzig which in 3 years has gone from 2.Bundesliga to the quarter finals of Uefa Champions League.

The Pyramids summer campaign made supporters dream, seeing for the first time in the club, names of a certain thickness: from Zamalek, a title contender every year, came the goalkeeper and the central defender of the National team: El -Shenawy and Ali Gabr, to which were added the Brazilian Rodriguinho, playmaker of Corinthians, Carlos Eduardo, striker of Goias, and finally Keno, offensive wing from Palmeiras, arrived for 9 million euros, a record for the African championships.

Undoubtedly the results were not long in coming (at the end of the season Pyramids in its first year will finish third in the league, gaining access to the CAF Champions League and will play the national cup final), but in September,

Turki Al-Sheikh announced that he had liquidated all of his investments in Egypt after a controversial episode. The Arab politician had told the press that he wanted non-Egyptian referees to direct his team's matches because he was afraid that the refereeing class would be pressured to favour Al Ahly. The Egyptian football association gave up on this kind of mediatic pression. This is the classic drop that makes the vase overflow. During a game of the Champions League, the ultras of Al Ahly heavily contest Al Sheikh and the Egyptian police intervene. This episode was a shock for the members of the league, while Turki Al Sheikh after a short period took back the lead of the Pyramids FC, he remains in the shadows until July and then definitively sell the club to an Emirate fund defining on its social channels the experience, "a pleasant experiment".

**A new chapter in Spain**

These words find consistency the following month when he unexpectedly announced the acquisition of the Spanish Segunda Division club Almeria. Currently the club is 6 points from the top of the League, thanks to unstoppable investments: Enzo Zidane, Coric from Rome and the talented 20 year old Uruguayan Darwin Nunez (current top scorer of the season). The ambitions of the frenetic Saudi Minister, now an entrepreneur, do not seem to stop here: he went viral when he invited Messi and Dybala to his Spanish villa last November to watch his Almeria match against Elche, he also asked Messi to play for his team.

Furthermore, in March he seems to have re-established relations in Egypt with Al-Alhy, returning as an honorary member. This leads back to the initial question, which is the only thought aroused by those who follow the events of the Saudi entertainment minister: What are Turki al-Sheikh's plans? And how far he wants to go?

Build an effective business model and use football as a soft power vehicle for Saudi Arabia. With good sports results, came also problems with awareness campaigns focusing on the situation of women in Saudi Arabia are increasing by many associations that work on civil rights. Al Sheikh responds to the questions that the Spanish media ask him and started a campaign that only increases the controversy. The final prize of the campaign was a new car and the winner was a Saudi woman. The day of the ceremony she showed up wearing a burka. The episode has rised questions that only the pandemic has silenced but not closed.

*Almeria's supporters cheers Al Sheikh - see.news*

The ability as a politician has allowed the Saudi Minister to be one of the most interesting and ambitious entrepreneurs, who has made some head-ons, then went to insert himself in a solid reality, as in Spain, facing new cultural problems. To date he is also president of the ISSF (Islamic Solidarity Sport Federation) which is responsible for ensuring cooperation, maximum understanding and a relationship of alliance and friendship starting from sports between all the states of the Islamic league. Surely he will still have to make a lot of mistakes, given his young age, but economic flexibility and his international football knowledge play a key role and will surely help him for the present and for his future challenges.

*Luigi Gemmi*

# *"UAE are better then England" said Amoory*

## *Omar Abdulrahman, the Maradona of the desert, the biggest talent in Arab Football in the last decade*

*Omar Abdulrahman with Al-Ain - thepeninsulaqatar.com*

Once upon a time there was a 21-year-old boy who was offered to go to work in England leaving the United Arab Emirates. An absurd offer, given that many managers and entrepreneurs crave the exact opposite, especially in times of crisis, given that we are talking about 2012. But in the world of sport, especially in football, some things work differently.

We are talking about a professional footballer: Omar Abdulrahman, known to his fans as *Amoory* . The destination was Manchester City coached by Roberto Mancini, while the club of origin was Al-Ain. Now we understand that it was not the offer that was absurd, but the failure to finalize the agreement. Officially, the failure to pass in the Premier League was due to the non-obtaining of the residence permit, but some rumors claim that the main reason was the high engagement required by the playmaker. Why would an Emirati footballer have to refuse the Premier League? Who is Omar Abdulrahman ?

**Everything for the family**

To begin with, Omar Abdulrahman was not always Emirati, since he was born in Riyadh, the capital of Saudi Arabia. But not for this he was Saudi: in fact he belongs to the *Hazrami* ethnic *group* , since her family originates in the Yemeni region of *Hazramaut* . For this reason Amoory and his family were foreigners in all respects, in the city where they lived and worked: a situation no different from that of many immigrants in Europe and America.

The first naturalization opportunity came with the Saudis of Al Hilal, the most famous club in the country, ready to register him. The young Omar declined the proposal because it did not include his family: a choice that gives the idea of the character of the footballer, who has shown to put his family ahead of his career. In fact, Al Ain's approach was different: the Emirate of Abu Dhabi team offered Amoory to obtain Emirate citizenship for the whole family. So not only was the offer accepted, but in addition to Omar, Khaled and Mohammed, two of his older brothers, still in force at Al-Ain, were also registered.

*Omar and his brother Mohammed - sport360.com*

The debut in the first team took place when he was not yet eighteen: it was 2009 and in charge of the club there was the German Winfried Schäfer, in the UAE had already coached the Al Ahli in Dubai. His control of the ball, his assists led Amoory in no time to wear the number 10 jersey of Al Ain and the one of Emirate national team.

Omar took part in the 2012 London Olympics, and this is where we return to the failure to move to Manchester City. Amoory chose to remain a supernatural being among his (now) compatriots, rather than risk a possible flop in Europe. But we must not forget that it would have been a change of life in a very different context such as language, religion, mentality. And clearly he could not have brought his brothers with him to the court of Roberto Mancini. Failure to become a *Citizens was* certainly not just for football.

## The Legend of UAE Football

Omar becomes an institution at Al-Ain: in 10 seasons he plays 231 games scoring 62 goals and serving 115 assists. He wins 4 championships, 4 National Cups and 3 Super Cups locally, while with the National team he triumphs in the 2013 Gulf Cup and reaches the semi-finals of the Asian Cup in 2015 after beating none other than Japan.

It seemed that Amoory would remain for his entire life at Al Ain, but  in August 2018 what you don't expect happens: the move to Al Hilal , the first club that had looked for him many years before. It is true that it was a loan for a year, but at a cost of 17 million US dollars! The investment did not pay off because after only two months the player ended the season prematurely due to the rupture of an anterior cruciate ligament. Unfortunately it was the third time, after the same injuries in 2009 and 2011.

Operated in Barcelona by Professor Ramon Cugat (trusted luminary of the Blaugrana club), he skipped the Asian Cup (of which he played the 2011 and 2015 editions) where he was eagerly awaited, also because in 2019 it was played in the United Arab Emirates. Once healed, he went on a free transfer to Al Jazira, another Abu Dhabi team. As he approaches the age of thirty, Omar Abdulrahman remains one of the most representative football players in Asia, he also has been renamed 'The Maradona of the Desert'. This is demonstrated by his presence on the podium of the Best Asian Player Award from 2015 to 2017, winning the award in 2016, after losing the AFC Champions League final against Jeonbuk Hyundai Motors.

Omar Abdulrahman has been the most crystalline Arab football talent of the last decade and we wonders what he would have been able to do in Europe. But by now it is too late and the best that Amoory had to offer seems to have already passed also due to the injuries that have hampered it. For football fans around the world, Omar's class and talent will be something to observe from afar, like a mirage in the desert.

*Javadi Saman*

# The Best Teams of 2019

## Qatar National Team, Asian Cup Winner and Al-Hilal, the Asian Club of the Century

# *The Aspire Generation*

**Qatar became the Asian champion in 2019, a triumph created with the decennal work of the Aspire Academy in Doha.**

*Qatar winner of the Asian Cup 2019 - english.alaraby.co.uk*

During the Al Kass tv program, before the Asian Cup 2019 took place, Xavi Hernandez, at that time Al Sadd player in the Qatar Stars League, had been called to play a game on the predictions of the Asian Cup and, to the general amazement, he indicated Qatar as the winning team. Many claimed that the prediction was ridicolous and that Xavi had made it for the simple reason that he was playing in Qatar ... and perhaps for that reason he knew the potential of the players. In fact, on February 1, 2019, history is written in Abu Dhabi: Qatar beats Japan 3-1 with the goals of Almoez Ali, Akram Afif and Hatem and became champion of Asia for the first time in its history.

Not a casual victory, but the triumph of a compact and talented team, which until the final had not conceded a goal, beating along the path respected opponents, such as Saudi Arabia in the group stage (2 -0), South Korea of Son Hueng Min in the quarterfinals (1-0), while in the semifinal, Qatar crashed Alberto Zaccheroni's hosts of the United Arab Emirates 4-0, in a boiling and hostile stadium given the political tensions within the Gulf area between Qatar and the other states, primarily UAE and Saudi Arabia.

The victory in the Asian Cup has also taken on a value of political struggle, not just sport. The protagonists of this historic success were undoubtedly the Spanish coach Felix Sanchez, who led this generation of players starting from the youth teams, and  the offensive couple, Akram Afif and Almoez Ali, the first leader of the assists, the second top scorer of the event with 9 goals, broke the record of goals in a single edition of the Asian Cup. Qatar wrote the story, thanks to the work of its youth generation and the Aspire Academy, a result that was unthinkable four years before, when the national team was made up by foreigners from South America and Africa.

## Qatar of South Americans and Africans

In the 2015 Asian Cup held in Australia, the Qatari national team, led by the Algerian Djamel Belmadi, badly ended the event with three defeats in the group stage against United Arab Emirates (4-1), Iran (1-0) and Bahrain (2-1). That National Team was a mix of players who grew up in Qatar (but actually born in North African or Middle East countries) and naturalized ones, like Boualem Khoukhi (born in Algeria), Trsor Kangambu (Democratic Republic of the Congo), Karim Boudiaf (France ) and Mohammed Muntari (Ghana).

Qatar has attempted to increase the value of its squad by exploiting the FIFA rules for naturalization. In view of the qualifications for Russia 2018, the Uruguayan coach Jose Daniel Carreno has recalled the compatriot Sebastian Soria as well as the Brazilians Rodrigo Tabata and Luiz Junior, the French goalkeeper Claude Lecomte and the Portuguese defender Pedro Miguel. All of them, together with the veterans of the 2015 Cup, Boudiaf and Muntari, went to form an almost totally "foreign" eleven, closer to a club team than to a traditional national team

The Qatari national team did not manage to improve, Daniel Carreno was succeeded by his compatriot Jorge Fossati, but at the same time, the disappointment of the Qatari public increased, especially towards the South Americans in the squad. After the lost match against Iran, valid for the qualification in Russia, the BeInSports broadcaster has taken a young fan out of the stadium to protest against foreign players, accused of lack of commitment. The video quickly went viral on the internet, highlighting an unknown national pride.

On the occasion of the last two qualifying matches, Jorge Fossati resigned and Felix Sanchez took his place, the spanish previously was in charge of the National U-19 and U-23 of Qatar. A decision that led to a drastic change, with the Generation Aspire who replaced most of the foreign players.

## The growth of young talents

In 2004, in Doha, the Aspire Academy was inaugureted, a colossal project created by Al Thani royal family: the largest football training center in the Middle East, which trained the greatest talents who won the Cup in 2019, such as Almoez Ali, Akram Afif and Bassam Al Rawi. After 15 years of work, one of the youngest and most exciting teams on the Asian scene was born.

The Aspire facility is located in Doha Sports City, a huge sports city in the shadow of the Qatar Torch Tower, a 300-meter-high Olympic torch-shaped palace inaugurated for the Asian Games that took place in Qatar in 2006. The academy includes a 50,000-seat stadium, the largest indoor sports center in the world (which includes an athletics track, a soccer field and a parquet floor for gymnastics), four Olympic-sized swimming pools, and a huge number of gyms and football pitches. A cutting-edge facility that has also been used in the winter retreats of some top European clubs, such as Bayern Munich, Juventus and Milan.

The Aspire Academy mission is to scout and train the best football talents of Qatar, creating for them a path that can lead them to have an outlet in professionalism in the local league and in Europe. In fact, the best Aspire Academy talents have the opportunity to complete their training process in Europe at some clubs owned by the fund that manages the academy, such as Kas Eupen in the Belgian first division, Lask Link in Austria, and Cultural Lioness in Spain.

TheTorch Tower near the Aspire Academy -pintarest.com

However, the project was not without controversy, given that, in particular 'Aspire

Dream', it deals with recruiting young talents from other countries into the Academy, to make them citizens of Qatar and therefore naturalize them when they have not yet reached the age of majority. Not surprisingly, the Asian Cup top scorer, Almoez Ali, is of Sudanese origins, while the defensive center Bassam Al Rawi is Iraqi. Qatar has therefore been accused of stealing promised young players from other countries.

## An impressive path of growth

The successes of Qatar start from far away, and the Aspire representatives have distinguished themselves in various youth tournaments. Starting from 2012, the Academy organizes the Al Kass international Cup, an Under 17 tournament that saw the hosts triumph in the 2014 and 2016 editions, beating Real Madrid on both occasions.

In October 2014, a few months before the National Team ended the Asian Cup with zero points, a new generation of players, the first formed by the Aspire project, led by Felix Sanchez, won the Asian Cup U19, after beating North Korea 1-0 in the final with Akram Afif's goal. Ali Almoez was also part of that selection, while Al Saadi and Moein, respectively top scorer and MVP of the event, in the end were unable to make the leap into the senior national team.

In 2016, Qatar hosted the U-23 Asian Cup, valid for qualifying for the London Olympics. The team, coached by Felix Sanchez, went very close to the glory, losing in the semifinal against South Korea, and also missing the goal of third place after losing the consolation final against Iraq. Despite this, Ahmed Alaeedin, the Egyptian striker who scored six goals and who is currently part of the national team, won the top scorer award.

Two years later, in the 2018 U-23 Asian Cup held in China, Qatar reached the semifinals again, losing this time against Vietnam (this time however it won third place against South Korea). After the triumph in U-19, the names of Akram Afif and Almoez Ali returned to the limelight scoring respectively 3 and 6 goals, showing an impressive maturity.

## The main talents of Qatar

The Qatari champion of Asia who will participate for the first time in the 2022 World Cup is a team full of young talents who have grown up among the Aspire Academy and who have the potential to perform well in Europe, starting from minor leagues.

The absolute protagonist of the 2019 Asian Cup was Almoez Ali, born in 1996, playing in Al Duhail a team where we also find the former Juventus players Mandzukic and Benatia. Ali was the top scorer of the continental event with 9 goals, setting a new all-time record of goals in a single edition of the Asian Cup, surpassing the 8 goals of Iranian Ali Daei in 1996. Qatar also took part in the 2019 Copa America and Almoez Ali, scored a stunning goal in the tie for 2-2 against Paraguay.

The last two editions as the best Asian player (among those militants in the AFC championships) went to two Al Sadd players, in 2018 to left back Abdelkarim Hassan, a player with explosive strength and a great shot from distance, plays the role in a modern way. Akram Afif, Almoez Ali's attacking partner in the national team, won the 2018/19 Qatar Stars League championship, scoring 26 goals and serving 15 assists. His great creativity and speed of execution allowed Al Sadd to reach the semifinals of the AFC Champions League in 2019 and for this reason he was awarded with the prize of best player of the year.

*Akram Afif and Almoez Ali -afc.com*

Definitely interesting and young is the defensive couple of Qatar, made up by Bassam Al Rawi and Tarek Salman. The first, born in 1997, plays in Al Duhail, where he is growing alongside Mehdi Benatia. In addition to being an extremely attentive and diligent center, in the Asian Cup he proved to be a sniper, solving thanks to his goals on free kicks the matches against Lebanon and Iraq. Tarek Salman (22) is instead a skilled defender in setting the maneuver from behind, he has the technique of a midfielder, skills that are the result of his years spent between the youth teams of Real Sociedad and Alaves in Spain.

This Aspire generation now, after conquering the Asian continent, must prove itself in Europe and leave the comfort zone of the local championship in order not to risk wasting its talent. The clubs should let the best talents move to Europe, in the Aspire-affiliated clubs such as Kas Eupen and Lask Linz in the first divisions of Belgium and Austria respectively, and then attempt a further leap.

Just last January Almoez Ali, seemed to be very close to the transfer to Austria to Lask Linz, club in which he had already played in 2015, but the negotiation was missed at the last moment and

the striker of the Qatari national team, remained with Al Duhail. A player who may move to Europe next season is Akram Afif, who already belongs to Villareal. Before consecrating himself to Al Sadd the little Qatari wizard had played with Kas Eupen and Sproting Gijon, and the time has come for him to return to Europe.

Qatar has won the Asian Cup, but to do well in the World Cup, as demonstrated by the last edition of Copa America, they need much more, they need a further leap in mental quality that this young and talented generation cannot achieve by remaining in the comfort zone of the Qatar Stars League. The national teams of Iran, South Korea and Japan, for years now have been the most competitive on the Asian continent given that the main talents, from a very young age, play in the European championships. Qatar must be able to do the same so as not to see the magnificent work done so far crumbling.

*Gineprini Nicholas*

**Quarter-finals**

| Date | Time | Team A | Score | Team B |
|---|---|---|---|---|
| 24 Jan,19 | 17:00 | VIETNAM | 2-1 (0-0) | JAPAN |
| 24 Jan,19 | 20:00 | CHINA P.R. | 3-2 (1-1) | I.R. IRAN |
| 25 Jan,19 | 17:00 | KOREA REPUBLIC | 1-0 a.e.t. (0-0,0-0) | QATAR |
| 25 Jan,19 | 20:00 | UAE | 0-1 a.e.t. (0-0,0-0) | AUSTRALIA |

**Semi-finals**

| Date | Time | Team A | Score | Team B |
|---|---|---|---|---|
| 28 Jan,19 | 18:00 | I.R. IRAN | 0-3 (0-0) | JAPAN |
| 29 Jan,19 | 18:00 | QATAR | 4-0 (2-0) | UAE |

**Final**

| Date | Time | Team A | Score | Team B |
|---|---|---|---|---|
| 01 Feb,19 | 18:00 | JAPAN | 1-3 (0-2) | QATAR |

**Group E**

| Team | P | W | D | L | F | A | GD | Pts |
|---|---|---|---|---|---|---|---|---|
| QATAR | 3 | 3 | 0 | 0 | 10 | 0 | 10 | 9 |
| SAUDI ARABIA | 3 | 2 | 0 | 1 | 6 | 2 | 4 | 6 |
| LEBANON | 3 | 1 | 0 | 2 | 4 | 5 | -1 | 3 |
| DPR KOREA | 3 | 0 | 0 | 3 | 1 | 14 | -13 | 0 |

| Date | Time | Team A | Score | Team B |
|---|---|---|---|---|
| 08 Jan,19 | 20:00 | SAUDI ARABIA | 4-0 (2-0) | DPR KOREA |
| 09 Jan,19 | 20:00 | QATAR | 2-0 (0-0) | LEBANON |
| 12 Jan,19 | 20:00 | LEBANON | 0-2 (0-1) | SAUDI ARABIA |
| 13 Jan,19 | 16:00 | DPR KOREA | 0-6 (0-3) | QATAR |
| 17 Jan,19 | 20:00 | SAUDI ARABIA | 0-2 (0-1) | QATAR |
| 17 Jan,19 | 20:00 | LEBANON | 4-1 (1-1) | DPR KOREA |

**Round of 16**

| Date | Time | Team A | Score | Team B |
|---|---|---|---|---|
| 20 Jan,19 | 15:00 | JORDAN | 1-1 a.e.t. (1-1,1-0)2-4 PSO | VIETNAM |
| 20 Jan,19 | 18:00 | THAILAND | 1-2 (1-0) | CHINA P.R. |
| 20 Jan,19 | 21:00 | I.R. IRAN | 2-0 (2-0) | OMAN |
| 21 Jan,19 | 15:00 | JAPAN | 1-0 (1-0) | SAUDI ARABIA |
| 21 Jan,19 | 18:00 | AUSTRALIA | 0-0 a.e.t. (0-0,0-0)4-2 PSO | UZBEKISTAN |
| 21 Jan,19 | 21:00 | UAE | 3-2 a.e.t. (2-2,1-1) | KYRGYZ REPUBLIC |
| 22 Jan,19 | 17:00 | KOREA REPUBLIC | 2-1 a.e.t. (1-1,1-0) | BAHRAIN |
| 22 Jan,19 | 20:00 | QATAR | 1-0 (0-0) | IRAQ |

# Al-Hilal: the asian club of the Century

**The Saudi Team that, with international player like Giovinco and Gomis, has won the 2019 edition of the AFC Champions League**

*Al-Hilal winner of the 2019 Champions League - bna.bh*

The current Al Hilal assistant coach, the Italian Diego Longo , defined, in an interview released some time ago, the *Al-Za 'īm* , nickname of the Riyadh team , as the *Real Madrid of Asia:* 15 times winners of the Saudi Professional League , 8 times winners of the National Cup, 2 Super Cups, 13 Crown Prince Cup and expecially 3 AFC Asian Champions League .

**Al-Hilal in mass culture**

Al-Hilal has always been one of the most successful and ambitious teams in the entire Asian football scene; in 2009, was defined by the prestigious research body IFFHS ( *International Federation of Football History and Statistics* ), as "Asia's Club of the Century ". The team currently perfectly represents the ambitions of the Saudi government more than ever interested in claiming and demonstrating, with heavy

investments, its role within the international football arena. During the last Club World Cup, the squad coached by Razvan Lucescu , son of the unforgettable Mircea Lucescu, has achieved a more than decent fourth place, it is, yet another clear confirmation.

Since its foundation on October 16, 1957, it has been considered a symbol and pride for 31 million people, also becoming one of the very first Asian teams to be able to "afford" the purchase of footballers and coaches from the *Far West* : Roberto Rivelino, Brazilian winger with Italian origins, considered the inventor of the famous footwork commonly known as 'elastic', wore the Al-Hilal jersey for 4 years, with moderate success, between 1978 and 1981.

Matteo Spatafora , the current athletic trainer of the team has repeatedly stressed the political "weight" of the team, interested, as never before, in investing to allow, not only, an exponential growth in the level of Saudi football, but also to make the Arabian Peninsula again attractive and irresistible in the eyes of potential foreign investors. The cornerstone of this ambitious project was "laid" way back in 2015 when Al-Hilal signed an important partnership with Unesco in order to further relaunch its image in the eyes of the world. 1.5 million dollars invested to give a very different and hopeful future to the children who live in one of the most complex and difficult areas of the Arab world.

To tell the truth, the company's HQ have always shown great interest towards the subordinate classes: by donating 25% of the proceeds of the games played in the home stadium, the majestic King Fahd International Stadium , to charity, organizing events in support of the most needy during *the Id al-fitr period* (the second most important festivity in the Arab world), and always doing everything possible to create an alternative narrative to the one presented in recent years by Western Media.

*The great coreography of Al-Hilal supporters - twitter.com*

The most felt challenge of the entire Arab football macrocosm is the match between Al-Hilal and Al-Ittihad, the symbolic teams of the megalopolises of Riyadh and Jeddah, both very popular at national level, both always "united" by a historical rivalry that, over the years, has always given great spectacle and emotions. The *Saudi Super Clasico* has seen in recent years a not indifferent dominance of Al-Hilal which in December 2009, further emphasized its superiority by overcoming the opponents with an astonishing 5-0. The protagonists of the victory: the Swedish Chirstian Wilhelmsson (former AS Rome) with a brace and the Brazilian Thiago Neves author of a *hattrick* , will not be easily forgotten ...

**Giovinco and Gomis: the faces of the Al-Hilal champion of Asia**

The purchases, which took place in recent years, of Sebastian Giovinco, Batefimbi Gomis (taken from Galatasaray for €6million), "*the cobra*" André Carrillo (arrived from Benfica for an amount close to € 10 million), which are added to a block Saudi with a not indifferent talent, they made Riyad's team an authentic war machine, capable of facing any challenge, both nationally and internationally. *"I have rarely found such an alchemy inside a squad"* : words of coach Spatafora, who was more than ever enthusiastic about the environment created around the team. The winger Salem Al-Dawsari, born in Jeddah in August 91', is the absolute idol of Al-Zaʿīm supporters. Its origins (it is indeed difficult if not impossible to find another Saudi footballer of this level on the international scene), and its style of play, unpredictable as well as effective, did the rest.

Al-Hilal managed to win the last edition of the Asian Champions League against Urawa Red Diamonds in the final. The Saudi team put an end to the domination of the East Zone after 7 uninterrupted years of success, but also dispelled the curse of the finals. In fact, between 1986 and 2017, 4 historic defeats arrived one step away from the coveted Continental Trophy: the 2014 Asian Champions League final is still in the memory of fans, the sensational double confrontation against the Australians of the Western Sydney Wanderers, in which despite the technical-physical superiority demonstrated in the 180' of the game, the Saudis were defeated 1-0 (decisive Tomi Juric's goal currently at CSKA Sofia ).

In 2017, however, the defeat in the final occurred against the Japanese side Urawa Red Diamonds, who drew 1-1 in Riyadh and then won in the fiery Saitama Stadium 1-0, with both goals scored by the Brazilian striker Rafael Silva (now at Wuhan Zall). Just last year, Al-Hilal took revenge on Urawa in the replica of the final of two seasons before. Lucescu's team landed on the final act of the tournament after beating the bitter rivals of Al-Ittihad in the quarterfinals, while in the following round they defeated Al-Sadd, the qatari side of Xavi Hernandez .

The first leg was played as in 2017 in Saudi Arabia, and this time *Al-Zaʿīm* did not concede a goal, winning 1-0 thanks to Peruvian Andrè Carrillo's goal. Giovinco and his companions were not intimidated by the seething Saitama Stadium, in the return match, and the *Atomic Ant* dispensed assists for the two goals of the victory signed by Bafetimbi Gomis and Al Dawsari.

The *French panther* , of Senegalese origins, former star of Lyon and Galatasaray, has not yet tired of scoring and has won the title of top scorer of the Asian Champions of 2019 with 10 goals that have also earned him the recognition of *MVP* of the Tournament. Sebastian Giovinco, the former star of Juventus and Parma, has finally reached continental glory after losing the Champions League final in North America with Toronto. Giovinco became the third 'Azzurro' (between players and coaches), after Marcello Lippi and Jacopo La Rocca, to raise the prestigious AFC Champions League.

**The most successful club in Asia**

With the success of 2019, Al-Hilal is the only Asian club to have won 3 editions of the Champions League together with the Koreans of Pohang Steelers . The Saudis can also boast of being the most titled team in Asia with 7 AFC titles: in addition to the 3 Champions, Al-Hilal has also won two Asian Cup Winners' Cups (1997 and 2002) and two editions of the Super Cup (1997 and 2000), events which unfortunately are no longer held today. The Al-Zaʿīm have also triumphed for two consecutive years, 1994 and 1995, in the Arab Club Champions Cup, an event that we could define as the Champions League of the Arab world, which includes teams from the Arabian Peninsula and North Africa. Al-Hilal last participated in the 2018/19 edition, losing the final (yet another) against the Tunisians of the Étoile du Sahel .

Despite the more than ever justifiable *ups and downs* , it can now be said with founded certainty: Al-Hilal has risen again and has everything it needs to continue to amaze and entertain millions of fans from all corners of the world.

*Accorroni Eduardo*

## Al-Hilal Asian Trophies

3 AFC CHAMPIONS LEAGUE (1991, 2000, 2019)

2 ASIAN CUP WINNERS CUP (1997, 2002)

2 ASIAN SUPER CUP (1997, 2000)

## Most successfull clubs in Asia

1° AL HILAL (SAUDI ARABIA) - 7 Trophies

2° SUWON BLUEWINGS (SOUTH KOREA) - 5 Trophies

3° POHANG STEELERS (SOUTH KOREA)
  SEONGNAM (SOUTH KOREA)
  AL ITTIHAD (SAUDI ARABIA)
  THAI FARMER BANK (THAILAND)
  AL QUWA AL JAWIYA (IRAQ)
  KUWAIT SC (KUWAIT) - 3 Trophies

# *Atlas of names Arabic football*

*In the round of 16 of the AFC Champions League 2017, the Al-Ahli of Saudi Arabia faced the Al-Ahli of the United Arab Emirates. Understand and remember names of Arab football clubs is really confusing sometimes, so we have created a simple guide to give you an orientation on the meanings of this fascinating language and learn the differences between teams with similar names*

## Al-Ahli: The Family

It is probably the most common name among Arab-speaking countries, whose meaning is "the family". Among them there are numerous teams, all noteworthy, such as the Saudi team located in Jeddah winner of 3 Saudi Pro League or the Doha Qatariots and then the Emirati Al-Alhi Dubai (now known as Shabab Al-Alhi Dubai) where in the past the world champion Fabio Cannavaro was hired as a coach. Probably the most famous Al-Ahli in the world is based in Africa, Egypt (Al-Ahly), the team who has won 8 times the Champions League

## Al-Shabab: Juventus

The newly founded club 2017 Shabab Al-Alhi Dubai, winner of 7 championships and 9 cups of the president, has been reborn with the name "Shabab" which is nothing more than what for Italians is Juventus: 'The young guys'. The Saudi Riyadh team, who had a glorious past, has the same name of UAE Team. 6 championships can be counted for the Saudi team between 1991 and 2012. Starting from next season the talented 32-year-old Argentine playmaker Ever Banega ex Valencia, Inter and Sevilla will join the club.

## Al-Hilal: The Crescent

Literally translated from the standard Arabic "the crescent", it has a coat of arms faithful and consistent with the team's background. The team has the nickname of al Za'Im, (the leaders, as it is the most successful) is located in Saudi Arabia, it is here that the Italian star Sebastian Giovinco currently plays and is the holder of the AFC

Champions League. Within the Asian federation there is another team under the following name from Palestine (Hilal Al-Quds FC)

# Al-Nassr: Victory

Al-Nassr or Al-Nasr: between the two transcriptions there is a very subtle difference which is explained in the geographical location. The first name usually corresponds to the team of the Gulf Monarchy, current holder of the Saudi championship, while the second is associated with the neighbours countries, we remember the Al Nasr of Dubai, Oman and Kuwait. The UAE Team has reached a good level but still too far from the Saudi homonymous. In all variants the name means "victory".

# Al-Jazira: The island

Often transliterated into Jazeera, it is a frequent and curious name in the Arab world. The most famous teams are those belonging to the United Arab Emirates, where the best local talents currently play: Ali Mabkhout and "the Maradona of the Desert" Abdulrahman. Also Amman in Jordan is another club with the same name. The meaning is literally "the island". The most famous Arab TV station has the same name and it has been repeatedly stressed that the choice fell on it as it claims to be the only independent news network in the Middle East.

# Al-Ittihad: United

The meaning of the name is "United", "doing it together". We can often read it in the most common Etihad transliteration, like the famous airline. Here too, the most famous and winning team is the Saudi one, winner of the AFC Champions League twice (2004 and 2005) to be added to the 17 different national titles between the King's Cup and the Championship. Here the legend Mohammed Noor has played for 18 years. Other teams with the same nominal body are in the UAE (Kalba), Bahrain and Syria.

*Gemmi Luigi*

# Number and Statistics for Clubs and National teams

## AFC Champions League

In total, the teams from the Arabian Peninsula have won 8 editions of the Asian Champions League: 5 Saudi Arabia, 2 Qatar and 1 the United Arab Emirates. The most titled club is Al-Hilal with 3 trophies (record shared with the Koreans of Pohang Steelers). With two successes we find the Al-Sadd of Qatar and the Saudis of Al-Ittihad, while with a single trophy, the emirates of Al-Ain.

Performances in the Asian Club Championship and AFC Champions League by club

| Club | Titles | Runners-up | Seasons won | Seasons runner-up |
|---|---|---|---|---|
| Al-Hilal | 3 | 4 | 1991, 2000, 2019 | 1986, 1987, 2014, 2017 |
| Pohang Steelers | 3 | 0 | 1997, 1998, 2009 | — |
| Esteghlal | 2 | 2 | 1970, 1990–91 | 1991, 1999 |
| Seongnam FC | 2 | 2 | 1995, 2010 | 1997, 2004 |
| Al-Ittihad | 2 | 1 | 2004, 2005 | 2007, 2017 |
| Jeonbuk Hyundai Motors | 2 | 1 | 2006, 2016 | 2011 |
| Urawa Red Diamonds | 2 | 1 | 2007, 2017 | 2019 |
| Maccabi Tel Aviv[2] | 2 | 0 | 1969, 1971 | — |
| Thai Farmers Bank[1] | 2 | 0 | 1994, 1994–95 | — |
| Suwon Samsung Bluewings | 2 | 0 | 2001, 2002 | — |
| Al-Sadd | 2 | 0 | 1989, 2011 | — |
| Guangzhou Evergrande | 2 | 0 | 2013, 2015 | — |
| Jubilo Iwata | 1 | 2 | 1999 | 2000, 2001 |
| Al-Ain | 1 | 2 | 2003 | 2005, 2016 |

The greatest Arab scorer in the history of the Champions is the Saudi Al-Shamrani, born in 1983, he's in the final stages of his career, he scored 32 goals in the maximum continental event (third in the all-time ranking) wearing the jersey of Al-Shabab, Al-Hilal, Al-Ittihad and even Al-Ain in the United Arab Emirates. Despite the huge amount of goals, Nasser Al-Shamrani has never won the Champions League. In second place we find the legendary Yasser Al-Qhatani with 18 goals. Forward who has 108 appearances for the Saudi national team, he lost the Asian Cup final in 2007 against Iraq and in 2014 and 2017 he lost the Champions League finals wearing the Al-Hilal jersey against Wester Sydney Wanders and Urawa Red Diamonds. In third place we find the Maradona of the Desert, Omar Abdulrahman, who lost the Champions League final in 2016 when he was at Al-Ain. Nowadays Omar Abdulrahman plays with Al-Jazira.

| Rank | Player | Club(s) | Goals |
|---|---|---|---|
| 1 | Lee Dong-Gook | Jeonbuk Hyundai Motors | 37 |
| 2 | Dejan Damjanović | FC Seoul, Beijing Guoan, Suwon Samsung Bluewings | 36 |
| 3 | Nasser Al-Shamrani | Al-Shabab, Al-Hilal, Al-Ittihad, Al Ain | 32 |
| 4 | Elkeson | Guangzhou Evergrande, Shanghai SIPG | 29 |
| 5 | Shinzo Koroki | Kashima Antlers, Urawa Red Diamonds | 26 |
| 6 | Ricardo Goulart | Guangzhou Evergrande | 25 |
| 7 | Muriqui | Guangzhou Evergrande, Al-Sadd | 20 |
| 7 | Asamoah Gyan | Al Ain, Al Ahli Shanghai SIPG | 20 |
| 7 | Youssef El-Arabi | Al-Hilal, Al-Duhail | 20 |
| 7 | Kim Shin-wook | Ulsan Hyundai, Jeonbuk Hyundai | 20 |
| 11 | Leandro | Gamba Osaka, Kashiwa Reysol Al-Sadd, Al-Rayyan | 19 |
| 11 | Adriano | Jeonbuk Hyundai Motors, FC Seoul | 19 |
| 13 | Yasser Al-Qahtani | Al-Hilal | 18 |
| 14 | Omar Abdulrahman | Al-Ain | 17 |
| 14 | Gao Lin | Shanghai Shenhua, Guangzhou Evergrande | 17 |

## Cup Winners' Cup and Super Cup of Asia

Both competitions no longer exist after the 2002 reform which led to the birth of the Champions League and the AFC Cup. In the two events, which joined the Asian Champions Cup, only Saudi clubs triumphed among those of the Arabian Peninsula and in both cups, Al-Hilal is the only one to have won it twice by sharing the record with Suwon Bluewings (Super Cup) and Yokohama F. Marinos (Cup Winners' Cup)

## Arab Champions League

Over the years, Saudi clubs have also dominated the Arab Champions League with 8 titles, while Qatar has only collected one. The Arab Champions League is an annual event held between clubs in the
West Zone of AFC and North Africa, such as Morocco, Egypt, Algeria and Tunisia. The most successful club this time is not Al-Hilal, but the Esperance de Tunis and the Iraqi Al-Rasheed.

**Performances by club**

| Num | Club | Winners | Runners-up | Years won | Years lost |
|---|---|---|---|---|---|
| 1 | Espérance de Tunis | 3 | 2 | 1993, 2009, 2017 | 1986, 1995 |
| 2 | Al-Rasheed | 3 | 0 | 1965, 1986, 1987 | — |
| 3 | Al-Hilal | 2 | 2 | 1994, 1995 | 1989, 2019 |
| 4 | Al-Shabab | 2 | 1 | 1992, 1999 | 1998 |
| | CS Sfaxien | | | 2000, 2004 | 2005 |
| 6 | Al-Ettifaq | 2 | 0 | 1984, 1988 | — |
| | ES Sétif | | | 2007, 2008 | |
| | Wydad Casablanca | | | 1989 | 2008, 2009 |
| 8 | Club Africain | 1 | 2 | 1997 | 1988, 2002 |
| | Al-Ittihad | | | 2005 | 1987, 1994 |
| 11 | Al-Ahly | 1 | 1 | 1996 | 1997 |
| | Raja Casablanca | | | 2006 | 1996 |
| | Al-Shorta | | | 1982 | |
| | WA Tlemcen | | | 1998 | |
| | Al-Sadd | | | 2001 | |
| 13 | Al-Ahli | 1 | 0 | 2002 | — |
| | Zamalek | | | 2003 | |
| | USM Alger | | | 2013 | |
| | Étoile du Sahel | | | 2019 | |

Al-Hilal won two titles like Al-Shabab and Al-Ettifaq, while Al-Ittihad only won the event once as Al-Ahli. Qatar's only victorious club in the Arab Champions League was Al-Sadd

# AFC Cup

The AFC Cup is an event reserved for clubs of the nations who do not automatically qualify a team in the Champions League groups. You will not find Saudi or Qatari clubs, but Kuwait, Jordan and Syria ones

Of the 16 editions of the Cup, 14 have been won by Arab Clubs. The most successful nation was Kuwait with 3 successes from Al-Kuwait and one from Al-Qadsia. Another team to have won the AFC Cup three times are the Iraqis of Al-Quwa Al-Jawiya, the only club to have done so for three consecutive years. There are three club successes from Jordan, with 2 Al-Faisily wins and one Shabab Al-Ordon wins. Two Syrian successes by Al-Ittihad and Al-Jaish, while Bahrain has won only once with Al-Muharraq. Last edition was won for the first time by a Lebanese club, Al-Ahed, who beat the North Korean April 25 in the final.

**Performances in the AFC Cup finals by club**

| Club | Winners | Runners-up | Years won | Years runners-up |
|---|---|---|---|---|
| Al-Kuwait | 3 | 1 | 2009, 2012, 2013 | 2011 |
| Al-Quwa Al-Jawiya | 3 | 0 | 2016, 2017, 2018 | |
| Al-Faisaly | 2 | 1 | 2005, 2006 | 2007 |
| Al-Qadsia | 1 | 2 | 2014 | 2010, 2013 |
| Al-Muharraq | 1 | 1 | 2008 | 2006 |
| Al-Jaish | 1 | 0 | 2004 | |
| Shabab Al-Ordon | 1 | 0 | 2007 | |
| Al-Ittihad | 1 | 0 | 2010 | |
| Nasaf Qarshi | 1 | 0 | 2011 | |
| Johor Darul Ta'zim | 1 | 0 | 2015 | |
| Al-Ahed | 1 | 0 | 2019 | |

The greatest Arab scorers in this event were Jordanian Mahmoud Omar Shelbaieh and Bader al-Mutawa (Kuwait) who scored 34 and 30 goals respectively, making them second and fifth in the All Time standings. Curiously, however, neither of them has ever won the AFC Cup. Moving slightly further north is the Iraqi Amjad Radhi, with 32 goals, winner of the three consecutive AFC Cups with the Al-Quwa Al-Jawiya.

**All-time top goalscorers**

| Rank | Player | Club(s) | Goals |
|---|---|---|---|
| 1 | Bienvenido Marañón | Ceres–Negros | 35 |
| 2 | Mahmoud Shelbaieh | Al-Wehdat | 34 |
| 3 | Aleksandar Đurić | Geylang United, Singapore Armed Forces, Tampines Rovers | 32 |
| 3 | Amjad Radhi | Erbil SC, Al-Quwa Al-Jawiya | 32 |
| 5 | Bader Al-Mutawa | Qadsia SC | 30 |
| 5 | Rico | Al-Muharraq, Al-Riffa, Al-Hidd | 30 |
| 7 | Ali Ashfaq | Club Valencia, New Radiant, VB Sports Club | 29 |

# Gulf Cup

The most important event in West Asia, in which only the 8 nations of the Gulf area participate: Saudi Arabia, UAE, Qatar, Kuwait, Oman, Bahrain, Iraq and Yemen.

The biennial tournament whose foundation dates back to 1970 has been won 10 times by Kuwait, but Al-Azraq has not won the event since 2010. The 70s and 80s were the golden era in Kuwait's football history , with the victory of 6 Gulf Cups, the success in the Asian Cup in the 1980 home edition at the expense of South Korea, and above all the participation in the World Cup in Spain in 1982.

| Team | Winners |
|---|---|
| Kuwait | 10 (1970, 1972, 1974*, 1976, 1982, 1986, 1990*, 1996, 1998, 2010) |
| Saudi Arabia | 3 (1994, 2002*, 2003) |
| Qatar | 3 (1992*, 2004*, 2014) |
| Iraq | 3 (1979*, 1984, 1988) |
| United Arab Emirates | 2 (2007*, 2013) |
| Oman | 2 (2009*, 2017) |
| Bahrain | 1 (2019) |

As we can see from the table, the Gulf Cup is synonymous with Kuwait. All seven other teams have won the Cup at least once, except for Yemen. 2019 was the first time for Bahrain, with the Dilmun's Warriors led by the Portuguese Helio Sousa who beat Saudi Arabia in the final.

The biggest scorer in the history of the Gulf Cup still in activity is the Emir striker Ali Mabkhout with 13 goals, he is also the best scorer in the history of his national team with 60 goals. The Gulf Cup all time scorer is from Kuwait and we are talking about Jasem Yakoub, for a total of 18 goals, he was the top scorer of the 1974 and 1976 editions (with 6 and 9 goals respectively) who saw on both occasions Kuwait wins the Cup. Special mention also for the Kuwaiti national striker Faisal Al-Dakhil, who scored 14 goals in the Gulf Cup which he won 4 times. Faisal Al-Dakhil is however well known for his brace in the 1980 Asian Cup final won 3-0 against South Korea, and for also scoring a goal against Czechoslovakia in the 1982 group stage of World Cup in Spain.

| | Player | | Country | | Goals |
|---|---|---|---|---|---|
| 1 | Jasem Yaqoub | | Kuwait | | 18 |
| 2 | Majed Abdullah | | Saudi Arabia | | 17 |
| | Hussein Saeed | | Iraq | | 17 |
| 4 | Jasem Al Huwaidi | | Kuwait | | 14 |
| | Faisal Al-Dakhil | | Kuwait | | 14 |
| 6 | **Ali Mabkhout** | | United Arab Emirates | | 13 |
| | Mansour Muftah | | Qatar | | 13 |

# Waff Championship

The biennial tournament founded in 2000 brings together all the teams from West Asia, not just those from the Arabian Peninsula. The event was often snubbed by the big names of the Peninsula, Saudi Arabia took part in only 3 of the 9 editions held, Qatar 2 and the Emirates, none. In this Cup we also find countries like Syria, Jordan, Lebanon and Palestine and also Kazakhstan and Kyrgyzstan took part one time each.

Iran is the most successful team in the Waff Championship having won 4 of the 10 editions. The last edition held in 2019 was won by Bahrain. Dilmun's Warrior 1-0 defeated Iraq that hosted the Cup.

| Team | | Titles |
|---|---|---|
| | Iran | 4 (2000, 2004*, 2007, 2008*) |
| | Iraq | 1 (2002) |
| | Syria | 1 (2012) |
| | Bahrain | 1 (2019) |
| | Qatar | 1 (2014)* |
| | Kuwait | 1 (2010) |

# Asian Cup

In the top competition for Asian nationals, there are 3 wins for Saudi Arabia (the last in 1996) and one for Kuwait, Iraq and Qatar. The Arab teams therefore won 6 of the 17 editions of the Asian Cup and on 5 occasions they reached second place in the event.

| Goals | Player | Representing |
|---|---|---|
| 14 | Ali Daei | Iran |
| 10 | Lee Dong-Gook | South Korea |
| 9 | Naohiro Takahara | Japan |
| | Ali Mabkhout | UAE |
| | Almoez Ali | Qatar |

The aforementioned Ali Mabkhout of the United Arab Emirates is the best Arab scorer in the history of the event with 9 goals over two editions. With 9 centers we also find the young Qatariot Ali Almoez, who led Qatar to the historic success of the 2019 Asian Cup by breaking the record of goals in a single edition that the Iranian Ali Daei had established in 1996.

# Asian Games

This competition is part of the Asian Olympic Games and has existed since 1951, four years before the birth of the Asian Cup. The event today, as well as football at the International Olympic Games, is reserved for U23 selections.

Of the 18 editions played, only two were won by Arab nations: in 1982 in India, Iraq triumphed in the final against Kuwait 1-0, while in 2006, the Qatar National Team who hosted the event won with a single goal against Iraq.

# AFC Footballer of The Year

| Year | Rank | Player | Team |
|---|---|---|---|
| 1994 | 1st | Saeed Owairan | Al-Shabab |
| | 2nd | Non-disclosure | |
| | 3rd | | |
| 2000 | 1st | Nawaf Al-Temyat | Al-Hilal |
| | 2nd | Hiroshi Nanami | Júbilo Iwata |
| | 3rd | Ryuzo Morioka | Shimizu S-Pulse |
| 2014 | 1st | Nasser Al-Shamrani | Al-Hilal |
| | 2nd | Ismail Ahmed | Al-Ain |
| | 3rd | Khalfan Ibrahim | Al Sadd |
| 2015 | 1st | Ahmed Khalil | Al-Ahli |
| | 2nd | Zheng Zhi | Guangzhou Evergrande |
| | 3rd | Omar Abdulrahman | Al-Ain |
| 2016 | 1st | Omar Abdulrahman | Al-Ain |
| | 2nd | Hammadi Ahmed | Al-Quwa Al-Jawiya |
| | 3rd | Wu Lei | Shanghai SIPG |
| 2017 | 1st | Omar Kharbin | Al-Hilal |
| | 2nd | Omar Abdulrahman | Al-Ain |
| | 3rd | Wu Lei | Shanghai SIPG |
| 2018 | 1st | Abdelkarim Hassan | Al Sadd |
| | 2nd | Yuma Suzuki | Kashima Antlers |
| | 3rd | Kento Misao | Kashima Antlers |
| 2019 | 1st | Akram Afif | Al Sadd |
| | 2nd | Alireza Beiranvand | Persepolis |
| | 3rd | Tomoaki Makino | Urawa Red Diamonds |
| 2005 | 1st | Hamad Al-Montashari | Al-Ittihad |
| | 2nd | Maxim Shatskikh | Dynamo Kyiv |
| | 3rd | Sami Al-Jaber | Al-Hilal |
| 2006 | 1st | Khalfan Ibrahim | Al Sadd |
| | 2nd | Bader Al-Mutawa | Qadsia |
| | 3rd | Mohammad Al-Shalhoub | Al-Hilal |
| 2007 | 1st | Yasser Al-Qahtani | Al-Hilal |
| | 2nd | Younis Mahmoud | Al-Gharafa |
| | 3rd | Nashat Akram | Al-Ain |

The following prize is a sort of Golden Ball for those players who play in the Asian championships and 11 times it has been won by Arab players, many of whom have already been mentioned in the course of this article. The most represented national team is Saudi Arabia with 5 triumphs, the last in 2014 with Nasser Al-Shamrani, the greatest Arab scorer in the history of the Champions League.

In the past two years, the recognition has gone to Qatari players, Abdelkarim Hassan and Akram Afif, both Al-Sadd militants and protagonists in the Asian Cup victory in 2019. Since 2012, the Asian international player of the Year has also been established, which goes to reward the best Asian footballer in Europe and no Arab has ever won this award that in the last few years is the domain of Son Hueng-min.

*Gineprini Nicholas*

[www.allasianfootball.com](http://www.allasianfootball.com) - Your Portal for Asian Football

*Social Media:* you can find us on Facebook, Twitter, Spreaker and Mixcloud

*Mail:* allasianfootball@gmail.com